92
1

D0828390

EYES

FRANKLIN WATTS

New York/London/Sydney/Toronto

© Franklin Watts 1990

Franklin Watts Inc
387 Park Avenue South
New York
NY 10016

Editor: Helen Broxholme
Design: K & Co
Consultant: Dr. Philip Sawney
Illustrations: Aziz Khan
Phototypeset by Lineage, Watford
Printed in Belgium

Photographs: Allsport 19t; courtesy of the Department of Education, NSW, Australia
29bl; Chris Fairclough 29br; Mike Galletly 4t, 5t, 18b, 22 (all); Robert Harding Picture
Library 5br, 18t; National Medical Slide Bank 15tr, 16t, 23tl, 23tc; courtesy of
Silhouette 5c, 21br; Science Photo Library 7b, 9t, 10t, 10br, 12t, 20 (all), 21t, 21bl, 23tr,
24 (both), 25, 27; John Watney (cover), 4br; ZEFA 14t, 14bl, 14br, 15t, 15b, 16bl, 16br,
19c, 19b.

Library of Congress Cataloging-in-Publication Data
Ward, Brian R.
    Eyes / Brian Ward.
        p.   cm. — (Health guide)
    Summary: Describes the construction of the human eye and discusses
problems with sight, infections, and injuries and how these may be
corrected with eyeglases or medicines.
    ISBN 0-531-14071-7
    1. Eye—Diseases and defects—Juvenile literature.   [2. Eye—
—Juvenile literature.   [1. Eye.]   I. Title.   II. Series.
RE52.W37   1990
617.7—dc20   90-31225
                                                                    CIP AC

CONTENTS

FEELING GOOD

Vision is one of our most important senses. As long as there is light to see with, our eyes constantly feed back information about our environment to the brain. Eyes are important to us in other ways. When you look at someone, or look at a picture of a person, your own eyes automatically look at the eyes of the person you are seeing. Even a tiny baby who can see very little, stares fixedly at its mother's eyes. Later on, when a child first tries to draw a face, the eyes are the first thing he or she will add to the shaky circle that represents the face.

▽ The iris of the eye is colored with melanin, the substance which gives skin a brown coloring. Brown eyes contain a lot of melanin. Eye color is inherited from our parents.

▷ Asian people have folded eyelids which protect their eyes from strong sun.

Albino people *(bottom right)* have no melanin in their eyes, hair and skin.

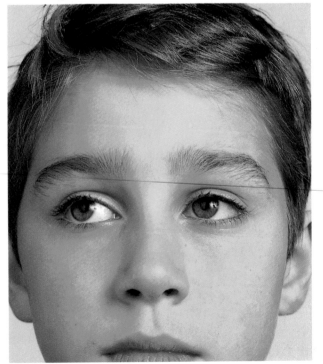

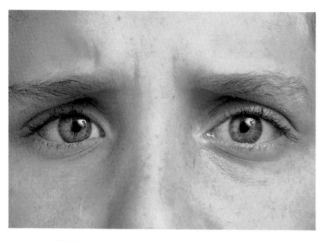

◁ Blue eyes mean that there is little melanin pigment in the irises. Blue eyes are common in people of North European descent.

Green eyes *(below left)* are unusual. Some people obtain this effect by wearing colored contact lenses.

▽ Eye makeup emphasizes the features we consider to be attractive. Cosmetics make the eyes look larger, and help draw attention to them.

Without our being aware of it, the pupils of our eyes open wide when we are looking at someone we find attractive. Knowing this, many painters exaggerate the size of the pupils in a portrait, to make the picture seem more attractive.

The importance of emphasizing the eyes as a way to look more attractive has been understood for thousands of years. The ancient Egyptians, Indians, Chinese, and Greeks used eye makeup and today, various types of makeup are used to draw particular attention to the eyes.

LOOKING AT THE EYE

Each eye is a ball, about an inch (2.5 cm) in diameter. It fits into the bony eye-socket, and is rotated by the action of six muscles. The eye is protected from shocks by a pad of fat behind it, and from other damage by the bony ridge above it. Most of the eye is covered by a whitish coat called the sclera. The front of the eye, called the cornea, is a transparent window which allows light to enter and reach the light-sensitive retina at the back of the eyeball. The cornea is the only living part of the body which does not have its own blood supply, as this would reduce the amount of light that could enter the eye. The cornea is very delicate, and is constantly washed and cleaned by antiseptic tears, produced from a gland at the edge of the eye. The eye-lids close in a blink to protect the eye from damage, or to spread tears evenly across the surface of the cornea.

▷ This section shows the structure of the human eye. Light enters the eye through the pupil and then passes through the lens which focuses it onto the retina. Information from the retina is passed to the brain along the optic nerve.

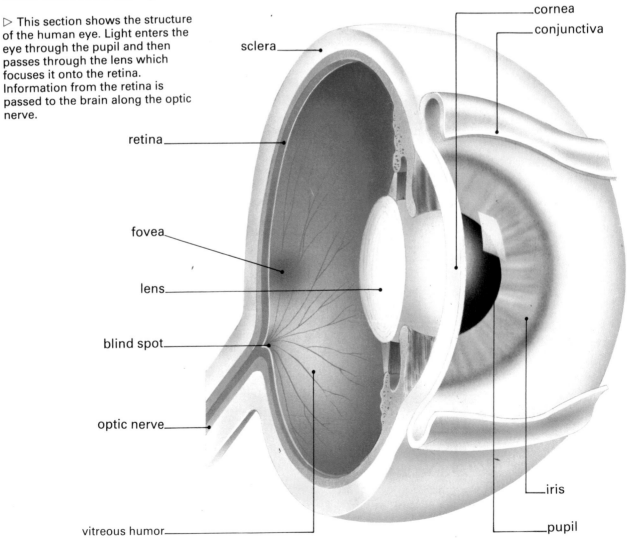

▷ The eyeball is moved in its socket by six muscles which work together in pairs. Each pair of muscles moves the eye in two opposite directions. When one muscle of a pair pulls, the other relaxes. The first pair moves the eye away from the nose and toward it, the second moves the eye up and down, and the third rolls the eye clockwise and counterclockwise.

▽ All of the major structures of the eye can be seen in this cross section.

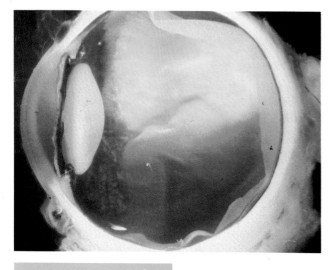

Just below the cornea is the iris, which is the colored part of the eye. Muscles in the iris regulate the amount of light entering the eye and passing through the lens just behind. The eye is mostly filled with a clear jellylike substance called vitreous humor. This helps to keep the spherical shape. At the back of the eye, leading off from the retina, is the optic nerve which carries visual signals to the brain, where a "picture" is produced.

HOW THE EYE WORKS

The basic operation of the eye is very simple. Light enters the eye through the curved cornea, and passes through the lens, which bends the light to focus a sharp picture on the retina at the back of the eye. This is similar to the way a camera works. Light entering through the lens is bent, to focus a picture on to the film. But unlike a camera, the lens in the eye is flexible. It is surrounded by tiny muscles which can pull, making the lens thinner, or relax, to let it return to its original thickness. When the lens is thinner, we can see distant objects clearly. When it relaxes, we can see more sharply in close-up.

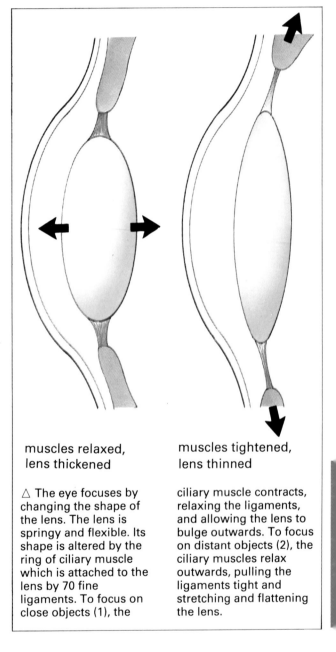

muscles relaxed, lens thickened

muscles tightened, lens thinned

△ The eye focuses by changing the shape of the lens. The lens is springy and flexible. Its shape is altered by the ring of ciliary muscle which is attached to the lens by 70 fine ligaments. To focus on close objects (1), the ciliary muscle contracts, relaxing the ligaments, and allowing the lens to bulge outwards. To focus on distant objects (2), the ciliary muscles relax outwards, pulling the ligaments tight and stretching and flattening the lens.

▽ When the lens is flattened and under tension, the eye can focus on objects more than 20 feet away. To focus on nearer objects sharply, the lens must be relaxed and bulging.

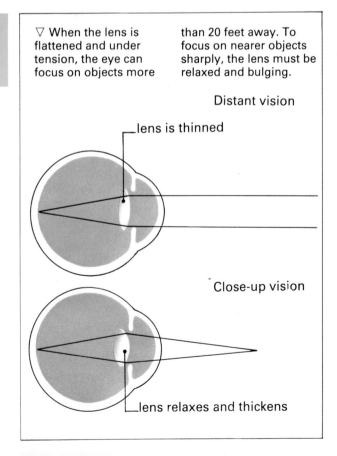

Distant vision

lens is thinned

Close-up vision

lens relaxes and thickens

We inherit the eventual color of the iris from our parents, but all babies are born with pale blue eyes. Some of these will change color as they get older.

Like photographic film, the retina works best with the proper level of light. The amount of light entering the eye is controlled by the colored iris. This is a ring of muscle that works automatically as light levels vary. In poor light, the circular iris opens wide to increase the size of the pupil so that extra light can enter the eye. In very bright light, the iris closes to a pinpoint, to protect the retina from glare. But signals from the nervous system can overide the effects of light. Although you are not aware of it happening, when you are scared or excited your pupils open wide, because they receive instructions from the brain.

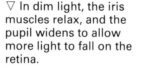

▽ In bright light, the muscles of the iris contract to narrow the pupil, and prevent damage to the retina.

▽ In dim light, the iris muscles relax, and the pupil widens to allow more light to fall on the retina.

△ Only half this iris contains strong melanin pigment, making one half brown, while the other half is blue.

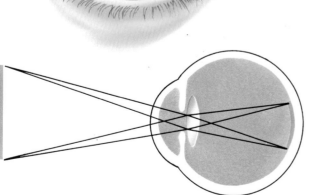

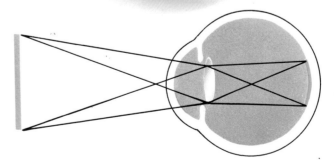

A clear image is formed, even when the iris closes

Light rays cross over as they pass through the eye

MAKING PICTURES

The most important part of the eye is the retina, where the image is received and transformed into tiny electrical signals which can be "read" by the brain. Buried in the retina are tiny sensory cells, each joined to a nerve fiber. These cells, called rods and cones, produce electrical signals when light falls on them. These signals are passed along the nerves to the brain, where they are "decoded" in the visual cortex to produce an "image" or picture. The nerve fibers bunch together and leave the eye through the optic nerve. The point on the retina where the optic nerve leaves the eye has no rod and cone cells. It is called the "blind spot."

▽ The brain processes the information received by our eyes. Electrical signals are passed to part of the brain called the visual cortex where they are decoded and made recognizable.

This is a retina (top right). The yellowish spot in the center is the blind spot, where the optic nerve leaves the eye.

This (bottom right) is a section through the blind spot. You can see the large optic nerve (stained red) leaving the eye.

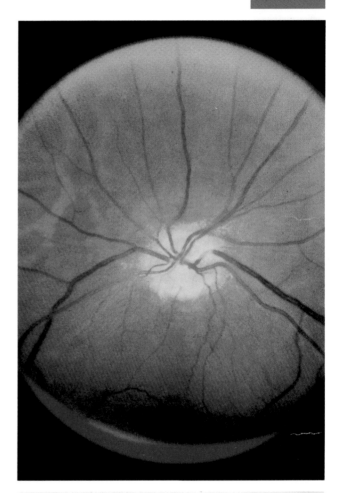

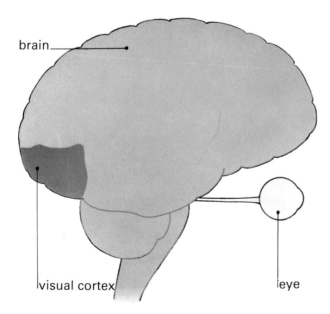

brain

visual cortex

eye

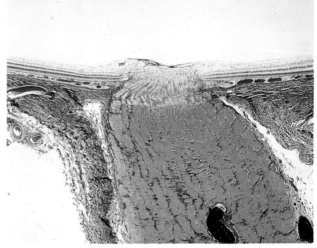

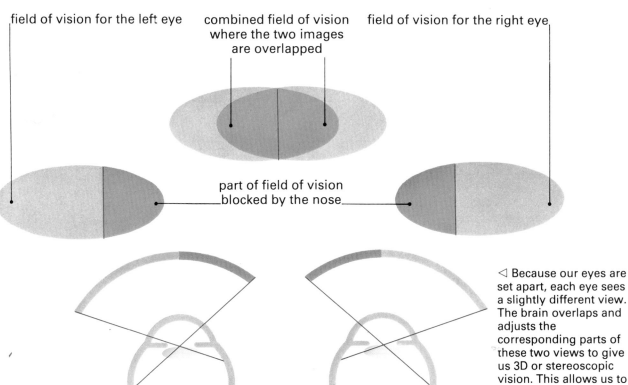

field of vision for the left eye

combined field of vision where the two images are overlapped

field of vision for the right eye

part of field of vision blocked by the nose

left eye

right eye

◁ Because our eyes are set apart, each eye sees a slightly different view. The brain overlaps and adjusts the corresponding parts of these two views to give us 3D or stereoscopic vision. This allows us to judge distances accurately. The outer ranges of our field of vision, where only one eye can see, is called peripheral vision. In these regions, the eye can only see movement and shadowy shapes.

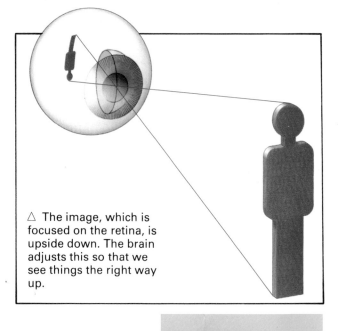

△ The image, which is focused on the retina, is upside down. The brain adjusts this so that we see things the right way up.

You can easily find your own blind spot. Draw two crosses on a piece of paper, about 3 inches (7.5cm) apart. Close your left eye. Then holding the paper up at arm's length, level with your eyes, stare at the left-hand cross. You will still be able to see the right-hand cross. But if you gradually move the paper closer, you should find that the right-hand cross disappears from the edge of your vision when the paper is about 8 inches (20cm) away. At that moment, the image of the cross is falling on the blind spot. Each of our eyes sees a slightly different image, because they are about an inch apart. The brain processes the two images, giving us 3D vision.

SEEING IN COLOR

Our color vision is made up of a mixture of colors from the cones, and sharp black and white images from the rods. If there is any error in the signals they send to the brain, the mixture of colors will be inaccurate, and a form of color blindness occurs. Many people are unable to distinguish properly between red and green, for example.

Another eye defect is a lack of sufficient rod cells, causing "night blindness" when light levels are low.

△ This photomicrograph of the retina shows the large yellow and green spots of cone cells arranged regularly across the surface. The smaller spots between them are the rods, which are much more frequent.

◁ The ganglion and bipolar cells and the rods and cones of the retina detect, process, and code into electrical signals each image focused onto the retina.

rod cells

surface of retina

cone cells

nerve cells leading to the optic nerve

light enters

▽ Color blindness affects 1 in 12 men and 1 in 200 women. The most common form is red-green color blindness which can be detected using the following charts. People with normal vision should see 2, 5, 6, and no number. People with red-green defects should see no number, 2, 5, 5 and people who are totally color blind should see no numbers at all.

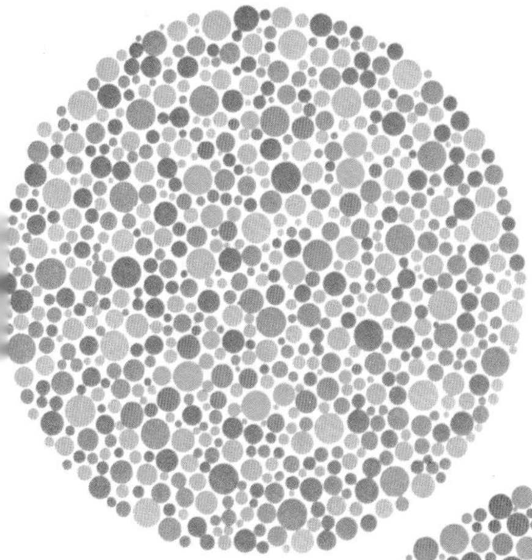

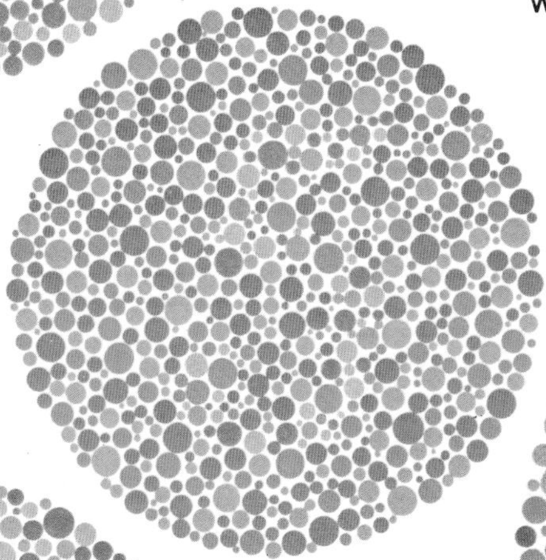

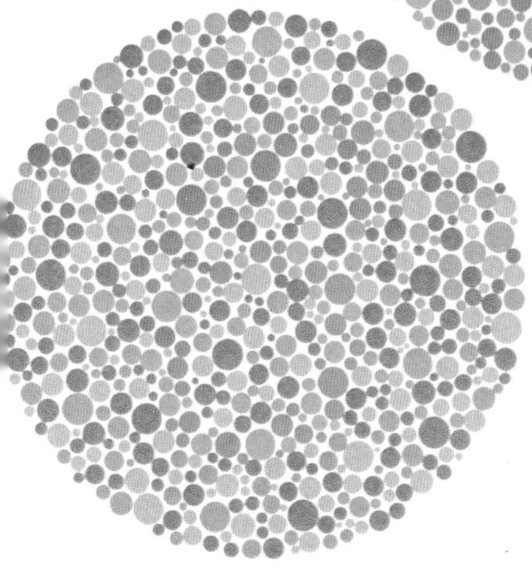

The rods and cones in the retina contain a purple pigment which is bleached almost immediately when light falls on it. It is this change in the "visual purple" that produces a nerve impulse. Rods are sensitive to very low levels of light, but they only produce an image in black and white. Cones are responsible for our seeing in color. They contain similar pigments, but these respond to either red, yellowish-green, or blue light. Cone cells only work in bright light. This is why, as dusk falls, the colors we see fade, until only the gray image produced by rods is visible. The rods and cones are closely grouped in a spot called the fovea, which is the point on which most of the light falls when we stare at something.

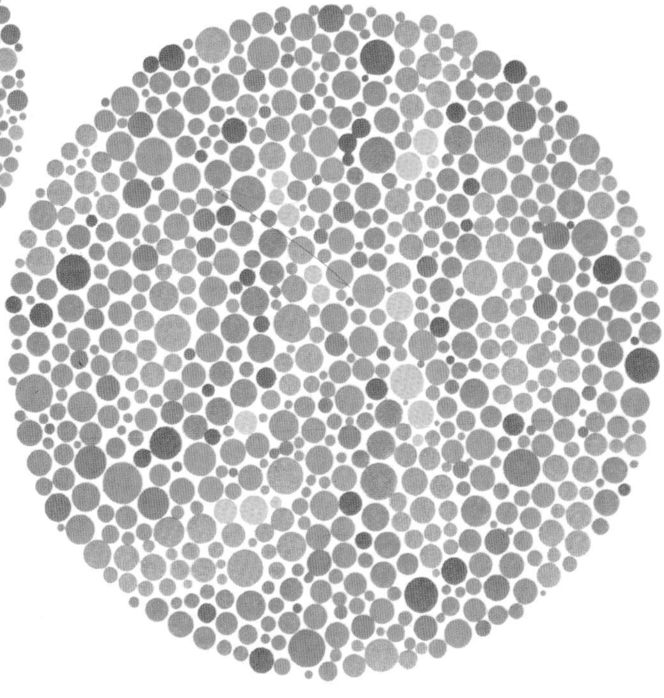

LOOKING AFTER EYES

△ Reading in bad light can strain your eyes. At the very least, it can cause headaches.

(Bottom right) Eye sight needs regular testing by an optometrist.

▽ Computer screens are produced in subdued colors to avoid eye strain and headaches.

Children normally have their eyes tested before they start school, and they need their eyes retested every year. Most people's eyes stabilize when they are adults, and so only need to be tested once every two years. If you already have defective vision, the optometrist will normally call you for a retest every year, in case your vision is changing. About 1 in every 5 school children have some form of visual defect, although most are only slightly affected.

Reading in poor light is often blamed for poor vision, but it is doubtful if this does, in fact, damage the eyes. Poor light is more likely to cause headaches, as is viewing too close to the television. Very bright light can cause eye strain; this is easily avoided with good sunglasses.

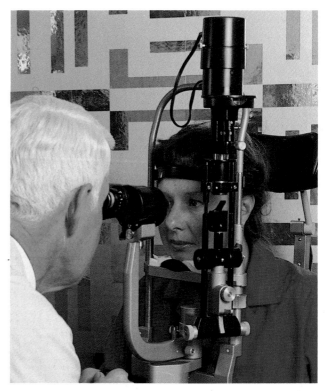

△ Using an instrument such as the one above, the inside of your eye can be examined.

Sunglasses *(top left)* eliminate part of the glare when the sun is bright. Some types are more effective than others, and you should ask the optometrist for advice.

◁ The greatest risk to sight is from damage to the eye itself, for example, during woodwork or chemistry, when damaging materials can get into the eye. Safety goggles must always be used if there is the slightest risk of anything damaging your delicate corneas.

SIGHT PROBLEMS

There are many possible eye defects, but the most common are nearsightedness (myopia) and farsightedness (hypermetropia). Both are caused by a defect of the curved front of the eye or the lens, which prevents the image being focused properly on the retina. In nearsighted eyes, the image is focused in front of the retina, so they can only see properly close up. In farsighted eyes, the image is focused on a point behind the retina, so they can only see well at long distances. Astigmatism is another common condition, in which the eye bends light irregularly, so that the image is wavy and blurred. Most people with mild eye defects can get by quite well. When the defect makes it difficult to see properly, some corrective lenses are needed. These lenses ensure that the light is bent and focused properly, restoring normal vision.

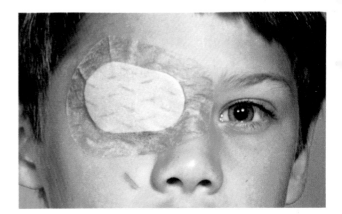

▽ Far-away objects appear sharply in focus to longsighted people, while those that are close appear blurred. *(Bottom left)* A nearsighted person can only see properly in closeup. Distant objects appear blurred.

△ A lazy or squinting eye doesn't move properly. As a result, the two eyes see in different directions. This can be caused by a fault in the nerve messages being passed to the muscles which move the eyes. Wearing an eye patch for a while can help.

Nearsightedness

Farsightedness

Astigmatism

Nearsighted eyes *(top)* focus the image of distant objects in front of the retina. This is corrected by wearing glasses or contact lenses with concave lenses.

Farsighted eyes *(middle)* focus the image of close objects behind the retina. This is corrected by wearing glasses or contact lenses with convex lenses.

An astigmatism *(bottom)* is caused by irregularities of the eyeball and is corrected by specially shaped lenses.

WEARING GLASSES

Many young people dislike the idea of wearing glasses, particularly when their sight problem is not serious. But once they do have glasses, they usually find that the benefits of being able to see well again far outweigh any inconvenience. Modern glasses are attractive, and there are many different styles of frame to choose from. Plastic lenses are very popular because they are light, although they tend to scratch easily. Glasses need not restrict anyone from any normal activities. Blurred vision in rain is now their only real disadvantage.

▽ The frames of glasses come in many different styles and colors. Some people like to wear "fun frames."

▷ Outrageous "fun frames" are a trademark of Dame Edna Everage.

19

◁ The frames and lenses of these special snooker glasses allow the player to see across the surface of the snooker table without having to raise his head.

▽ Eye problems need not hinder sport or other physical activities. Special glasses are available, such as these swimming goggles, which are fitted with prescription lenses.

◁ Sunglasses which protect the eyes from brilliant sunlight, can be decorative as well as practical.

CONTACT LENSES

Contact lenses are an increasingly popular alternative to glasses. These tiny, paper-thin lenses cling invisibly to the cornea. Unlike glasses, they provide normal all-around vision, and they also overcome the problems of smeary or steamed-up glasses. They need very accurate fitting, and the wearer must follow a strict cleaning process. This is important, as the lenses are in contact with the delicate cornea, and any dirt or contamination could cause eye infection.

▷ Hard contact lenses are less expensive than the soft types. But some people find they irritate their eyes and are less comfortable to wear than the soft ones.

△ Soft contact lenses suitable for extended wear are fragile and need careful handling and cleaning. Some types can be kept in the eye for up to 3 months.

◁ Most contact lenses are almost invisible in the eye, but with this hard corneal lens, you can see its raised edge.

Contact lenses are usually inserted daily. This is done by placing them on a clean fingertip, opening the eyelids wide, and delicately putting the lens in place on the cornea. Some people find this very difficult, and others are afraid that they might lose the lens under their eyelid. But with practice, the technique is quick and simple. A few people have very sensitive eyes, which cannot tolerate contact lenses for any length of time.

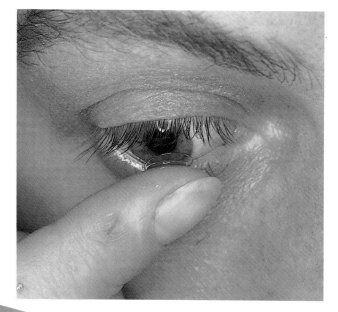

▽ When contact lenses are being fitted, a colored fluorescent dye is dripped into the eye to reveal how closely the lens fits to the shape of the cornea.

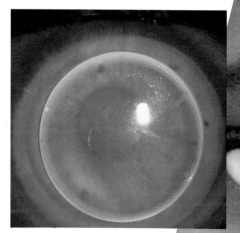

▷ Contact lenses can be worn for cosmetic and dramatic effects as well as for correcting sight problems.

EYE PROBLEMS

Watering and runny eyes are problems that affect everyone at some time. They can be due to an allergy like hay fever, or to the wind blowing into your face. They happen because the eye is producing tears faster than they can drain away. Production of cleansing tears is the natural reaction of the eyes to anything which irritates them. Tears drain from the eye through a small duct leading into the nose. Sometimes extra tears cause your nose to drip, too. If you have a cold, the ducts are sometimes blocked up and this also makes your eyes runny.

▽ The eyebrows, eyelids, and eyelashes protect the eyes from dust and injury.

▷ We blink automatically if anything comes too close to our eyes and to clean them.

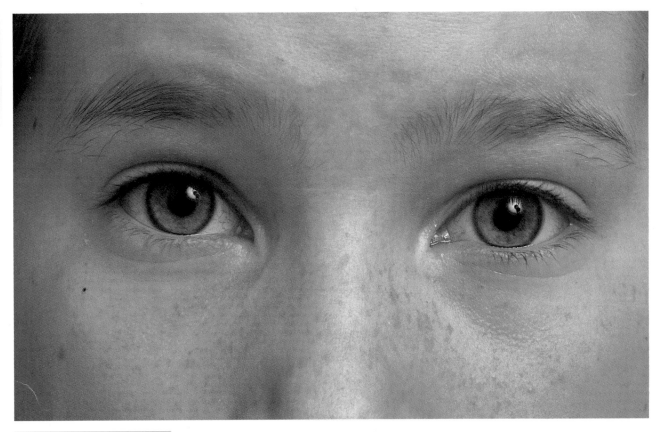

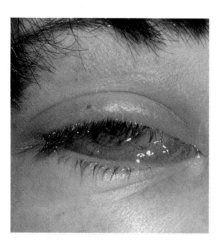

△ Conjunctivitis is an inflammation and reddening of the membrane which lines the underside of the eyelid and the outer parts of the "white" of the eye. It is sometimes caused by an allergy, but can also be caused by infection. Avoid spreading infectious conjunctivitis by careful handwashing and not sharing towels.

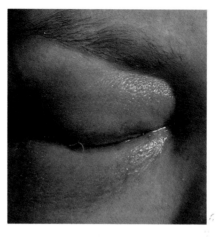

△ Some cosmetics cause a dramatic allergic reaction in the sensitive skin around the eyes. Using hypoallergenic cosmetics may prevent this.

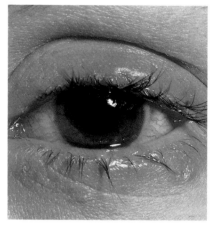

△ Blepharitis is a condition caused by inflammation of the edge of the eyelid. It usually starts as a form of eczema, but often becomes infected and weeping. Affected eyelids need careful washing, and medical treatment may be necessary.

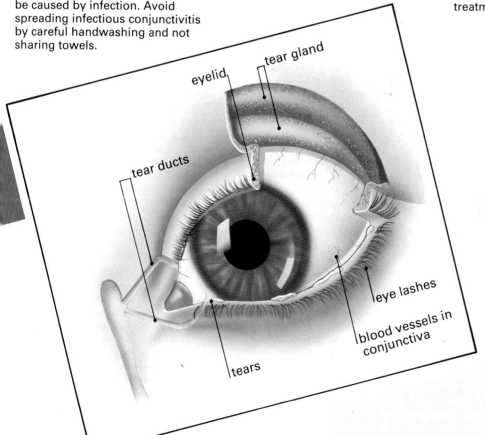

eyelid

tear gland

tear ducts

tear ducts

eye lashes

blood vessels in conjunctiva

tears

◁ Each time we blink, tears are washed over the delicate cornea and conjunctiva to stop them drying out, to wash away any dust particles, and to disinfect the eye. Tears are made in glands above the eyelid. Each blink squeezes tears from the gland across the surface of the eye and into the tear ducts. From the tear ducts, the tears collect in the tear sac and drain into the nose.

SERIOUS PROBLEMS

For such a delicate and sensitive organ, it is surprising how surgery can improve some serious eye problems. For example, glaucoma is a disease which is responsible for 13 percent of blindness. It is caused by a build-up of extra fluid in the eye. Normally, this fluid is drained through a channel in the iris. In glaucoma sufferers, the channel is blocked, causing a build-up of fluids in the eye which presses against the retina's arteries, cutting off its blood supply and causing blindness. It can be cured by a simple snip on the edge of the iris, usually done under anesthetic, which opens up the channel to let the fluid drain properly.

▽ Laser surgery for eye problems involves meticulous placing of the laser beam, using special instruments.

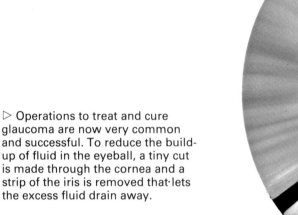

▷ Operations to treat and cure glaucoma are now very common and successful. To reduce the build-up of fluid in the eyeball, a tiny cut is made through the cornea and a strip of the iris is removed that lets the excess fluid drain away.

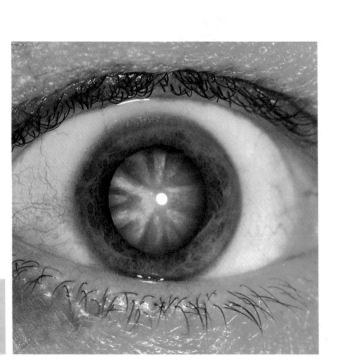

◁ Cataracts are caused by the lens of the eye gradually becoming opaque. At first, the vision is blurred, but it may become completely obscured. Cataracts are treated by surgical removal of the lens, after which almost perfect sight is restored by the fitting of a tiny artificial lens inside the iris of the eye, or by special glasses. Cataracts can be caused by aging or by some diseases.

Sometimes the retina becomes detached from the back of the eye. If the damage is slight, the retina can be tacked back into place by a laser. Otherwise, it can be stitched back, while the patient is under anesthetic. Most serious eye problems can be treated successfully, provided they are caught early enough. Even if an eye is damaged so badly that it must be removed, it can be replaced by an artificial eye which looks very realistic; however, it will not restore sight in that eye.

FIRST AID FOR EYES I

Proper first aid requires training, but as eyes are so easily damaged, it is sensible to learn some simple, emergency first aid techniques. The most important thing to remember is to act quickly and correctly, to prevent further damage which in some cases could mean loss of sight. After even the slightest damage to the eye, there is a natural reaction to rub it. This is the worst thing you can do, as it will only increase the damage. The cornea is very sensitive and the smallest speck of dirt on it will feel enormous. The eyes are self-cleaning, and they respond to any injury or irritation by producing floods of tears. These may wash the source of the irritation away, but you must still check the eye carefully to make sure that the damaging material has really gone.

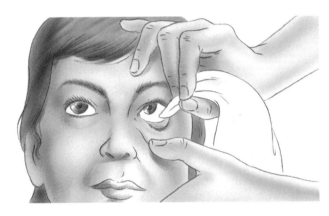

△ Then, taking the corner of a clean, damp handkerchief, try to lift the foreign body off the surface of the eye.
   Never attempt to remove a foreign body if it is on the pupil or the iris of the eye, or if the object is sticking into the eye. Trying to remove the object may damage the eye. Call for immediate medical help.

Removing foreign bodies

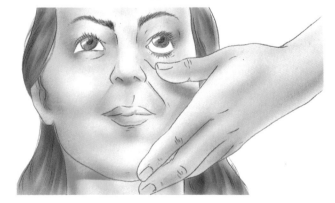

△ Eye injuries can be very serious. If anything damages the eyeball, infection and even blindness may occur. Foreign bodies, such as dust particles, often blow into and irritate the eyes, sticking to the wet surface.

Foreign bodies on the white of the eye and under the lower eyelid are easily removed. Tilt the person's head back and pull the lower eyelid outward and downward. Then ask the person to look up.

△ To remove an object from under the upper eyelid, ask the person to look down and gently pull the upper lid down and over the lower one.

Examining the eye

Treating a black eye

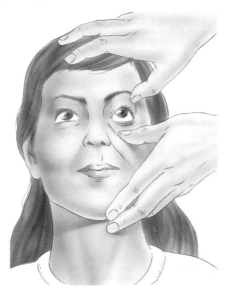

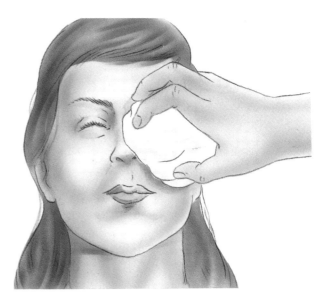

△ It is very important to examine the eye carefully, to assess any damage. Before you examine anyone's eyes, wash your hands. Ask the person to sit down in front of you, facing the light and with their head tilted back,

against you. Then, using the index finger and thumb of one hand, gently open the eyelids. Ask the person to look left and right, and up and down so that you can see every part of the eye.

△ Very little can be done to help a black eye. But the swelling can be reduced by applying a cold compress to the eye immediately. This can be made by wrapping ice cubes in a clean cloth.

The skin around the eyes is very delicate and is easily damaged. A black eye is a bruise of the eye. It is usually dark in color and very swollen, often forcing the eye to close up.

FIRST AID FOR EYES II

Bathing the eyes
◁ Sometimes, neither blinking extra water into the eye, nor using any of the methods described on the previous pages will remove an object from the eye or under the eyelids. Bathing the eye is often the answer.

Fill a jug with sterile water if possible, or with warm, salted tap water. Ask the person to sit on a chair and tilt his or her head toward the injured side. Pour water across the surface of the eye, letting it drain over the cheek and into a container.

Chemical burns
▷ It is very important to wash the eye if anything splashes into the eye. Corrosive chemicals can easily enter the eye and quickly attack its surface, causing severe damage and even blindness. Make sure that the person does not rub his or her eye as this will only increase the damage. Hold the affected eye open under a gentle stream of cold tap water, ensuring that water drains away from the uninjured eye. Call an ambulance to take the person to hospital immediately.

Dressing the eye

◁ All injuries to the eye need urgent medical attention. If you have been unable to remove a foreign body from the eye, or the eye has been damaged in any way, it is usually a good idea to dress the eye. This gives the eye extra protection and helps prevent further infection. Place a sterile eye pad over the eye and very gently bandage it in position. Be very careful not to bandage too tightly as this may damage the eye and cause unnecessary pain.

▽ Our eyes are very easily damaged and we must take great care of them. Racing drivers wear helmets with visors to protect their eyes from flying dust. Industrial workers should wear goggles to protect their eyes from bright light and flying debris.

FACTS ABOUT EYES

Blindness is very common in the poorer tropical countries. There could be as many as 20 million people world-wide who have become blind because of disease.

A "four-eyed" fish called an "Anableps," has eyes shaped like a figure eight. When it floats on the surface the water comes up to the center of its eye, so one part looks up above the water surface, and the lower half can see under the water.

People working with a computer all day often find that their eyes are very tired and they often get headaches. This is probably because they need to stare to read the blurred writing on the screen. Some people are concerned about the risk of causing cataracts or damaging the unborn baby, but these risks have not been proven.

Many animals have much sharper sight than humans, although most do not have good color vision. Hawks and eagles can see a tiny mouse hidden in the grass when they hover hundreds of metres in the air.

"Spots before the eyes" are usually things called "floaters." You can often see these if you stare at a blank wall or a piece of white paper. They are caused by small pieces of debris breaking away from the inside of the eye and floating in the aqueous humor around the lens. They are normally completely harmless, but if you find they are increasing greatly in number, you should consult your doctor or optometrist.

The retina of the human eye contains more than 120 million rods and 7 million cones.

A squint or cross eyes is caused when the eye muscles pull unevenly so the eyes do not track together as they move. Often very small babies have a squint, because they have not yet learned to control their eyes automatically. If the squint is still present a few years later, it can usually be corrected by special glasses and eye exercises.

When you look at a bright light for a while, you will "see" bright red or green color when you close your eyes. This is because the strong light has temporarily bleached the visual purple in the rod cells in the retina, so the only light messages reaching the brain are those from the cone cells which produce red or green images. The effects soon wears off (but don't stare at very bright lights or the sun for more than a few seconds, or you could cause permanent damage).

A lizard-like animal called a tuatera, living on an island near New Zealand, has a "third eye" in its forehead. This eye is not properly functional and its purpose is not understood. The tuatera is a "living fossil," and is distantly related to the dinosaurs.

Cats and birds, as well as other animals, have a third eyelid. This nictitating membrane helps to protect the eye. You can easily see this brown colored membrane in the eye of a sleepy cat.

A blink is a reflex action to clean the eye, and it happens without you having to think about it. If you try to stop yourself blinking, you will find it impossible to keep your eyes wide open for more than a couple of minutes.

GLOSSARY

Albino: Person (or animal) lacking the usual coloring substance in the skin, hair and eyes. Albinos have very pale pink skin, and pink eyes.

Allergy: A condition in which the immune system of the body reacts against some harmless substance as though it was dangerous. Allergies can cause runny and bloodshot eyes, sneezing fits, and skin rashes.

Antiseptic: Substance which kills bacteria and other microbes when it comes into contact with them.

Cataract: Condition affecting the lens of the eye, which causes it to become milky and can eventually cause blindness.

Cornea: The transparent front of the eye, which covers the iris and pupil.

Eczema: An allergic reaction which causes the skin to become inflamed and scaly.

Fovea: The part of the retina at the back of the eye where most of the rod and cone light receptors are grouped. The eye moves so that the maximum amount of light is focused on the fovea, to give very clear vision.

Hypoallergenic: Substance which is not known to be a common cause of allergy.

Inflammation: Reddening of a part of the body, as a reaction to an injury. Inflammation is caused by the body's defenses as they start to repair the damage.

Iris: The colored ring at the front of the eye.

Laser: Device which produces a very intense beam of light. It is used in eye surgery as a knife and as a welding torch.

Lens: The part of the eye that focuses light entering the eye on to the retina. It is nearly round, and is composed of layers of transparent cells, like an onion.

Melanin: The dark colored pigment which gives color to the iris, skin and hair.

Membrane: Very thin and fragile sheet of cells.

Nerve fiber: Fine thread attached to a nerve cell, along which nerve impulses or messages are passed very quickly.

Night blindness: Condition in which a person cannot see in dim light. It is usually caused by an absence of light-sensitive rod cells in the retina, which usually work in quite dark conditions.

Ophthalmoscope: Instrument used for eye examination. It works like a microscope, allowing the retina of the eye to be seen in detail.

Optic nerve: The short nerve carrying signals from the rod and cone cells in the retina to the brain.

Prescription lens: If you have poor eyesight which needs correcting, the optometrist will supply prescription lenses, either in the form of glasses or contact lenses. Prescription lenses are curved very precisely and individually so that vision is corrected.

Pupil: Small opening in the center of the iris, through which light enters the eye. The iris can open or close the pupil so the right amount of light falls on the retina.

Sclera: Tough, yellowish coating which covers and protects all of the eye except the area covered by the cornea.

Visual cortex: Part of the brain in which messages received from the eye are decoded to produce the images we see.

Vitreous humor: Clear, jelly-like material which fills most of the eye, so that it keeps its rounded shape.

INDEX

PRINTED IN BELGIUM BY
proost
INTERNATIONAL BOOK PRODUCTION